Additional Praise for *A Prayer of Six Wings*

It calls and it calls and it tears the heart. So precise, it's precise until it hurts. Here the prophet Joel comments on "from generation to generation", from the generation of the prophet 2500 years ago: About this to your children tell the story, to your children, to their children, to the generation after.
—YOSSI YZRAELI
Echos from the Cellar of the Contrabass

About "Remembering the Doves of Ma'agan":
I instantly loved "The Doves of Ma'agan . . . as I've been on Lake Kinneret in northern Israel, and felt how peaceful the ambience is there despite conflicts. I admired the gentle clarity of this poem and how it offers hope that I can almost taste.
—PASCALE PETIT
Tiger Girl
Judge, Poetry News (Poetry Society, U.K.) Winter Competition

As Owen Lewis says in his masterful, moving, and timely collection *A Prayer of Six Wings*, "I can't talk about Israel tonight…I can't not talk about Israel tonight." Many have been silenced by fear, and others are finding their voices, but few have been able to make "poetry" out of the horrific October 7th events, and their aftermath. From Owen's home turf on the Upper West Side of Manhattan where posters of the hostages were ripped down nightly, to his granddaughter's birthday party on Hahashmonaim Street, where sudden noises can be popped balloons or bombs falling, these poems of witness are both immediate, musical, and humane, as they ask, "How then, and when, can we imagine peace?"
—RICHARD MICHELSON
Sleeping as Fast as I Can

About "(from captivity) When living children":
In its divisions and joinings of words, a lyric voice has found a way to create a disordered language in which to render this new poem's subject as lived truth. This poet's empathetic imaginings, no matter their source, become a lyric cry on behalf of those whom the poem speaks of.
—MARCIA KARP
If By A Song
Judge of the 2024 E.E. Cummings Prize

A Prayer of Six Wings is lovely, sad, wide-ranging in its learning and mourning, devout without piety, prophetically angry, and most of all, steadfast in love of family and humanity.
—DAN BELLM
Practice: A Book of Midrash

A PRAYER
OF SIX WINGS

OWEN LEWIS

DOS MADRES
2025

DOS MADRES PRESS INC.
P.O. Box 294, Loveland, Ohio 45140
www.dosmadres.com   editor@dosmadres.com

Dos Madres is dedicated to the belief that the small press is essential to the vitality of contemporary literature as a carrier of the new voice, as well as the older, sometimes forgotten voices of the past. And in an ever more virtual world, to the creation of fine books pleasing to the eye and hand.

Dos Madres is named in honor of Vera Murphy and Libbie Hughes, the "Dos Madres" whose contributions have made this press possible.

Dos Madres Press, Inc. is an Ohio Not For Profit Corporation and a 501 (c) (3) qualified public charity. Contributions are tax deductible.

Executive Editor: Robert J. Murphy

Illustration & Book Design: Elizabeth H. Murphy
www.illusionstudios.net

Typeset in Adobe Garamond Pro & Lithos Pro
ISBN 978-1-962847-19-3
Library of Congress Control Number: 2025930069

First Edition
Copyright 2025 Owen Lewis
All rights reserved. No part of this book may be reproduced or transmitted in any form or by any means graphic, electronic or mechanical, including photo-copying, recording, taping or by any information storage or retrieval system, without the permission in writing from the publisher.
Published by Dos Madres Press, Inc.

GRATITUDE

My gratitude always to Fran Quinn, extraordinary teacher; to Robert Abrams and Greg Egan, always my first readers; and to so many friends and colleagues who generously read this book and helped it evolve: Dan Bellm, Joanna Chen, Elizabeth Coleman, Ilana Ganot, Jessica Greenbaum, Richard Michelson, Yehoshua November, Alicia Ostriker, Cindy Savett, Yerra Sugarman, and Yossi Yzraeli. I am indebted to Jessica Jacobs and the entire *Yetzirah* community, its "hearth for Jewish poetry" and for Jewish poets. Many members of this community heard earlier versions of these poems. To Rabbi Jeremy Kalmanofsky and his weekly parsha class at *Ansche Chesed*—many of the Talmudic sources in these poems derive from his teaching. Deepest thanks to Robert Murphy, publisher of Dos Madres, and Elizabeth Murphy, extraordinary book designer, who have shepherded my manuscripts into beautiful books and to Moshe Schulman who gave lift to this book's six wings. With the indulgence of my children Victoria Lewis and Hezi Ben Sasson, and my grandchildren, who have allowed me to tell a part of their story; and as always, to my wife Susan who nurtures and supports my writing.

*for the ordeals of the captives
and their families*

TABLE OF CONTENTS

Introduction - *Alicia Ostriker* viii

My Partisan Grief, SuperNova, October 7, 2023 1

At-home Coliseum, New York 3

Yochevet Lifshitz, age 85, released by Hamas,
    Reported N.Y. Times, Oct. 24, 2023 6

Visiting 8

In the Van to JFK 9

Remembering the Wedding, ... 11

A Belief in Order 12

After a Concert, New York 13

Overheard in a New York Restaurant 16

Five Minutes in Tel Aviv 17

Hamas Releases a Video, Reported N.Y. Times, Nov. 14, 2023 ... 18

Learning that 19

Independence Day, May 14, 1948 20

Not in the News 22

Obituary, Gideon Klein (1919-1945) 23

Remembering the Doves of Ma'agan (1973, 2024) 25

Obituary for a Forgotten Friend,
    Lost Between October 6-25, 1973 26

Negotiations, I'm Confused 29

Equation Revealed, First Release
    Reported N.Y. Times, Nov. 22, 2023 31

News from the Streets 32

On Redeeming Captives and a Little Known Islamic Midrash 33

Generation to Generation -*L'dor vador*..................................35

A Saturday Morning, Tel Aviv..36

Waiting for the Next Release
    Reported N.Y. Times, Nov. 23, 2023.............................37

From a Graveyard for Children,
    A Midrash on How G-d Stopped Crying.......................38

(from captivity) When living children...41

A Psalm of Celebration..43

A Nightmare of Friday Evening Services,
    (Three Israeli Hostages . . . Dec. 5, 2023)..........................44

Sabbath in Kurjenoff, 1901..46

Obituary, Avrum Miles (1943-2023)...47

Two Thousand Pound Bombs Drop,
    Reported N.Y. Times, Dec. 22, 2023.............................48

Shame...50

Weaponized Sexual Violence on Oct. 7,
    Reported N.Y. Times, Dec. 29, 2023.............................52

A Lesson for the Jubilee Year..53

Interrogation...55

Israeli Military Confirmed Pulling Thousands of Troops
    Out of the Gaza Strip, Reported N.Y. Times, Jan. 1, 2024......57

In a Dream...59

Conversation...61

Birthday...62

Community Garden, Riverside Park
    Free Gaza, Chalked on the Sidewalk...............................65

The Morning Call...66

Prospect Park Boat House, Brooklyn...67

116th & Broadway...68

My Namesake, An Understanding...71

If the Holy Land...73
Rosh Hashanah Seder, 2024 74
"Who will last, ...79
A Beach in Tel Aviv..80
Of Six Wings..81
Sutzkever's Last Words...82

Notes...85
Acknowledgements..93
About the Author 95

A PRAYER OF SIX WINGS

INTRODUCTION

A Prayer of Six Wings is an extraordinary book, not for the ideological but for the intellectually and emotionally engaged, and for lovers of poetry and truth. In the prophet Isaiah's vision, the seraphim attending God's throne possess six wings: two to cover the face, two the feet (possibly implying genitals), two to fly. In this study of trauma, born from the Israel-Gaza War, the poet's ego and personal history are, like an angel's, modestly underplayed. After reading in the New York Times of "Weaponized Sexual Violence on October 7," he notes of himself and his wife, "For weeks after, we avoid sex." Meanwhile the poet's violinist daughter rehearses for a concert in Tel Aviv. By the close of the book she has performed in Tel Aviv and New York a piece by a composer who died in the Shoah at age twenty-five, an age so many have died in the current war. The poet has a spritely granddaughter named Noa, and when he watches a video of a young woman named Noa violently taken captive by Hamas, we understand these are all our children. The poems travel between America and Israel, between the man tearing down posters of hostages in New York City and the "vast and unforgiving desert" where "there are not pebbles enough" to place on the twelve hundred graves, and a midrashic sky in which God "couldn't possibly hold all the dead children…and the closer he drew them in, the more He cried." These poems are very Jewish, but fly beyond the enmity of Jews and Palestinians to a deeper sense of "these my sons, these my cousins." When will there be healing? Is there comfort in distance? "Forty years, my friend. Our grandchildren's children's lifetimes. Not ours." For readers exhausted by the news and resistant to the righteous rhetoric of both sides in this war, Lewis' vital and elegant, humane and compassionate work will be embraced and treasured.

—*Alicia Ostriker*, 2024

Who will last, what will last? A wind will last.

~*Avrom Sutzkever*

My Partisan Grief, SuperNova, October 7, 2023

These are my cousins.
I don't know them. These
my sons, daughters, young lovers
and friends. I don't know them.

Their music fills the desert sky.
They dance to wed the Negev night.

Before dawn, the stars have fled. Those
watchful stars like angel eyes. *Who
silenced you angels? You've lost your song.*

The light is old and bitter
breaks the dark these
sudden sparks start at a rifle's

mouth. Mouth to mouth

silenced. What unsilenced rage
wrangles through ranging
hearts? Not glinted stars these

quicker knives quickening life-
exits.   What music now, here
in the vast and moving desert,

these vast and unmoving rocks,
this vast and unforgiving grief—

my cousins
my sons
my daughters.

At-home Coliseum, New York

The tv's looping on a 26 year old woman
named Noa as she's thrown onto a motorbike
straddle. She reaches
                        into my living room.
(I almost take her hand, again and

again our fingers *almost* touch—
                        just beyond
the glass—like that one second when
G-d supreme on the Sistine ceiling
touches Adam's finger to give him pulse.

No jolting there, no spasm, no cry-out,
no outcry: the first man gets breath and soul.

Or perhaps it was the moment just before.
They're both so calm, expectant, the everlasting

moment after moment) and now,
generations later,   Noa is hostaged

to all the memories buried
in the catacombs of civilization beneath
the many coliseums,
                        inside the tv set
in my living room.

*

In my living room, Noa, almost four,
is looking under the couch for the lion.
She's my granddaughter, and shapes
my fingers into a cage

enclosing the lion. She passes her hand
over its head like a blessing, declares it
asleep   *safe* for me to open the cage.
TV off, we play in front of its dark stare,

sitting on a couch that sits on a rug
on a floor over a basement, and below that
labyrinths of somewhere catacombs, tunnels
where the dead and the living plot. We play

finger games—cat and mouse, and pigs
going to some market, or churches
and steeples and open the doors
to all the praying peoples. So many

languages! We must be in the midst
of Babel's ruin. No one hears the other's
prayer. I hold up my index finger
to ask for a moment of silence.

Noa takes a quick breath, looks at me
expecting an explanation. I'm thinking,
"In Hebrew, the index is
the teacher."   Words failing,

my Noa, this Noa, rests her head
on my lap, the lion on hers.

I wait for the lesson of these days,
    or more than a lesson,   for all
days, all generations

                    (if there are to be
generations for all

Yochevet Lifshitz, 85, Released by Hamas, Reported N.Y. Times, Oct. 24, 2023

Excuse me for stepping into
your story but your married name
I couldn't ignore. My namesake,

Oscar Lifshitz, came from Kurjenoff,
near Minsk. We might've asked Oded,

your husband, if we're related, but he's
still in the captor's underworld. Why
did they release you? The tv

shows your release. The world watches: you
thank the captors with *Shalom*.

Do they know the name *Yochevet* (mother of
Moses, Aaron, and Miriam, with tambourines
dancing the women into songs of deliverance

as the Red Sea drowned Egypt's chariots.)
If the captors had understood your namesake
they'd have held you as agitator or spy. (Who

can imagine dancing these days?) Do you

pray to the G-d of Abraham
who appeared in the sound of a voice
that threatened the desert sky?

Nightly you pace your small living room
retracing your own steps that once ambled
the desert floor, that now ceilings

your husband's captivity.

Do your feet   hurt, your knees, your   hips?
Mine   ache, side-stepping this grief.

I avoid the many notes of condolence,
must write, each with pen, paper, and stamp.
Some have already returned: undeliverable.

You and I have in common
a name and I must visit as family
as soon as I can, as soon as I locate

the twelve hundred graves.

VISITING

in the desert
there are not pebbles enough.

I gather sand,   palmfuls,

and the wind carries them off.

IN THE VAN TO JFK

*(My daughter, her husband and children
have been out of Israel for six weeks.
I come along for an extra hour with them.)*

The van rides on suspended judgment.
The pot-holes shake loose my worries
for Victoria and Hezi (his arm across
my shoulders to comfort me), the young
Noa and Kobi, a paraphernalia caravan
of an exodus—strollers, car seats, bags.
I offer gingermen cookies. They wince.

We wince at the news from Tel Aviv with
its iron dome of science fiction. Earlier,
siren-lights exploded across the tv's screen.
There, sky-bombs in splinters of the sun,
the rush to shelter to avoid the hail of
falling missles. How long will the system
hold? Constant words of

annihilation, counter attacks. Wounded
pride of the leaders. In rhetoric's echo-
chamber of threat, people are sacrificed.
Homeless families torn like rags.
Survival passes into revenge.
(And may G-d protect our fraying souls.)

Back in Tel Aviv, no one wastes a single day.
My daughter, a violinist, resumes rehearsing,
calls me as she enters the hall's orchestra pit.

Tchaikovsky's second. The phone's still on, the musicians still tuning their petulant instruments when the conductor launches. Plaintive gives ways to agitation. *Piu presto!*

Where is he sending those notes?

Remembering Their Wedding, August 24, 2017

The *chuppah* flapping on a bluff over the Mediterranean
fills with the golden setting sun. I, too, was marrying

a new country, its dialects taken from the prayers
of grandparents for a future invented by grandchildren.

"Son-in-law," the word in Hebrew, *hatani,* my groom,
as if we were all gathered by *the laws of Moses and Israel*

to exchange rings of this timeless sunset light. Here,
my daughter married, and the Law of Return blessed us

with a metaphor whose reality is incomplete:
a watered orange-grove, a basket of unpressed olives,

a Sabbath bride waiting for the feast to begin. She holds
a cluster of grapes, pristine plums without "the print

of fingers." In her heartbeat, the Song of Songs;
        her vow, "I am my Beloved's, my Beloved mine."

A Belief in Order

My daughter returns
to bring music to a stunned
country, her orchestra straining
in every note—still echoing
halls once over-filled, once
Beethoven's tympanied Fifth.

I wanted to tell her be safe,
stay in New York. She knew all
I didn't say. If I hear missiles
she stays in their midst—to rally
the percussions, the clear voices
of a congregation of horns; flutes

luring frightened hoopoes back
to the singing banyans; dreaming
doves to the date palms; the strings'
full timbre seeking the autumn
garden's blue muscari, the field's
scented white saffron-crocus—

their necessary music that heals
even as it anticipates the wounds.

After a Concert, New York

There's a nightly violation:
the posters of hostages are torn,
cut down. Next day, sympathizers
tape them back, ever more securely,
and the Fall evening needles its cold
through my coat. (The concert

I just heard, erasing.) In the crosswalk,
the light flashes red—
                        the figure of a
man—Stop! A shadow moves, not a
shadow—who is he? Who rips the night,
tears the posters, the faces of hostages,
the face of young Yagil Jacob, age 12,

defaced; Shani Gore, age 29, eyeless,
Yaffa Adar, 85, with cut cheek,
her fierce look speaking to me:
Tell him!
          Is this ripping free speech?
Against the law? Where are the police?
I finger 911 on the phone.
                        Stop him

  before it's too late.
                And why don't I
speak up, stop him,
                put myself
between him and the hostages?

The light turns. I don't look.
We're side by side on the sidewalk,
Yaffa, from the poster, watching

me watching him.
                      Who *is* he?
More of him, across the street,
a stealth band splattering graffiti.
What are you doing? Will you keep us
hidden? We're already cut to pieces?
The tape securing Itzik Elgarate,

age 68, and Noam Or, age 17,
stronger,
         and another poster of
  Yaffa Adar staring at me
beneath the signs: 77th St. and
Broadway. Here in New York,
do I bring the fighting to this

street corner?   Does that
help?
    I look at him Yaffa's glare,
the red man in the walk-light
    embers
white,
      a war behind her eyes,

fury
    trapped beneath her skin;
her eyes,
        my eyes,

                his eyes staring
as he
      rips more of Yaffa away.

      With a pair of scissors
                          cuts her.

Dare me—his eyes
              demand—*Just*
  dare me!

Her eyes glare back.

Overheard in a New York Restaurant

"I can't talk about Israel tonight."

    "I know."

"I can't not talk about Israel tonight."

       "I know."

"Can we talk about . . ."

"Here?   Sure. Let's try to talk about here."

Five Minutes in Tel Aviv

"Dad, just give me a few.

    I'll call you
back in five. There's a siren.
    I need to find a safe room."

Hamas Releases a Video, Reported N.Y. Times, Nov. 14, 2023

claiming Noa Marciano is killed
by her own coutry's bombardment.
She pleaded by video with her country,

this 19-year-old colonel (how young
is she?) once on look-out,
the guard-tower, Kibbutz Nahal Oz.

In the next sequence: a body covered
by a sheet pocked red,
a rash of bloody bullet holes.

Now she's a plagued body
thrown to a fire. Bodies dead
and bodies embering.

The noon sun wanes
refusing its own light; heaven
eclipsing,   a river of blood lava,

houses like hills, buildings like mountains
explode outpourings on the streets
this magma flows and magnums

clot, this woman called Noa. This
and another and how many Noas
will be left? She bleeds into the sheet.

A generation's miscarriage.

LEARNING THAT

among
the many Israeli
dead, numbering
           125 at Kfar Aza, and
   among them,
              three babies butchered
strung on a wire
         like drying laundry.

INDEPENDENCE DAY
    MAY 14, 1948

And I was born   three years
and nine days after.   The next day
a war began. The mandates

drawn on cartesian maps
in the disappearing ink of Biblical claims:
roads, valleys, vineyards, alleys,

and from every chimney-pipe
the smoke of a new Palestine
and a memory of Europe.

Once, we were all Palestinian.

My crib had been readied
for three years and nine days. My mother's
many miscarriages passed through it

as if to mourn all the Shoah miscarriages
and all the Shoah children
flooding heaven. We needed time

for G-d to   sort the souls.

My grandmother sang a Yiddish lullaby
and everyone cried and
cried to bring laughter to my *bris*.

They tried Hebrew songs of the new pioneers,
the *halutzim*; laughed how much they still
sounded like Poland. They said I laughed, too.

We're all native speakers   of this sad laughter.

NOT IN THE NEWS

On October 7th, an ambulance dispatcher
answered the call of a desperate
mother—"I put my
           baby in the washing
machine.

        Look for him, listen for him.
   listen . . ." Then,

silence.

OBITUARY, GIDEON KLEIN (1919-1945)

After 1940 Gideon Klein, pianist-composer,
wasn't allowed to perform. The Nazis
wouldn't listen to Jewish interpretation but
lauded "Karel Vranek,"
                        until they transported him

to Terezín, December, 1941, age 22,
where he composed, played, directed
music to show the Red Cross inspectors
the Nazis' worth,
                        who again transported him

to Auschwitz on October 1, 1944, then
Fürstengrube, a coal mining work camp
to better use his composer-pianist's
trained hands.
                        Until murdered, two months

after completing the string trio. Twenty-five
years old. The score was left in Terezín,
hidden, protected.
                        Until performed in Prague,

June 6, 1946, when Klein's sister organized
the concert: Four Movements—Allegro,
Variations on a Moravian Folk Song,
Lento, Molto Vivace—modern, melodic,
haunting, almost forgotten.
                        Until again performed—

my daughter with fellow musicians in Tel Aviv
and New York. Each concert begins with her telling
his story. As if a relative, just lost, just fallen.
    His memory in music.

Remembering the Doves of Ma'agan
(1973, 2024)

A wing stretch, a single beat,
the tips of star-point vanish.
They brush off sleep like a kiss.
Their soft-lofting coos usher them
down from nests in the date palms
to the banks of the ancient Kinneret.

It's morning. They gather to watch
the lake-mist dancers present and
dancers past, what traces of grace left
to these waters. The doves drink slow
draughts, preen feather by feather, bird
by bird, and all are counted by stories in

the many languages ever spoken here,
syllable by syllable, word by word. Each dawn
is drawn in the history of water on the lips
of the shore, the lips of the men who've claimed
to own the shores. These, once birds of
peace, are the ones who carry its memory.

Obituary for a Forgotten Friend, Lost Between October 6-25, 1973

I had always intended to write about him,

        Dubie, or Dov.

It's July and August, 1973, a pediatric surgery rotation at Hadassah Hospital after a month on a kibbutz in the Kinneret. In the surgical theater, as intern, he was allowed to open the young patients, sometimes close them. I, a medical student, was allowed to hold retractors. Tedious hours for both, but his eyes above the surgical mask spoke patience for the many years of training ahead of us.

He brought me to the roof perched on Mount Scopus and we feasted on patient snacks, crackers and apple juice,

    in the Jerusalem evening.
    the sunset hills cooled,
    Mount Olivet, Mount Ophel,
    Mount Zion, and its golden
    song. I had always wanted
    an older brother.

He was leading a trip for The Nature Preservation Society into the Sinai, part of Israel since the 1967 Six Day War. On flatbed trucks, we traversed dry wadis for miles, explored wind sculpted caverns, climbed Mount Sinai at 3 am.

> The night sky in the Sinai
> so full of unknown stars,
> the whispered desert silence.

At the tip of the Sinai peninsula, Rosh Mohamed, the head of Mohamed, snorkling with

> schools of rainbow fish,
> their arching streaks of color,
> the Covenant's rainbow renewed.

All the while, he kept an eye on me. He'd douse me with water to remind me to drink. He was himself an oasis; I, a neophyte wandering this arid climate.

Returning to Jerusalem along the Gulf of Acqaba at midnight we all bathed

> in the phosphorescent surf
> washing our parched selves,
> tingling in the light of glowing
> waves, the lavender night,
> bodies in the iridescence—
>   I might still reach him.

~

I left Israel mid September that year, and on Yom Kippur, October 6, 1973, another war began. Sometime between that day and October 25th, Dov, a reservist, himself becoming   a surgeon, now called back to the army to fight . . . was he yet twenty-five? . . . and his body, beyond surgical repair.

I had always intended to write
about him.   I had always
intended to return sooner than
I had. Almost forty years
until I returned to the country
built on sand and desert land.

Negotiations, I'm Confused

and the trade-offs begin:
who's offering five hostages for
five days of bullets?

A pause in bombing for women,
children, the elderly, not for men?

(Who is Netanyahu, who Hamas?

Do they actually speak)
about the 54 Thai crop-workers
caught in the sudden crossfire?

Almost half the hostages hold foreign
passports from twenty-five countries.

The world watches.

Rifles, munitions, canons, tanks.
    (What is the equation?)
Swords into ploughshares

for water, for medicine, for fuel, and
for soldiers' bodies. (What fuels
the promises?) In the sky's

flurry, levant's cast
of sparrowhawks and drones
watching drones, eyes on

the dusty trails of convoys
and caravans, Hagar's path
and Ishmael's thirst. For him,

a skin of water when he left,
forsaken. For his cousins,
a snowfall of manna.

Amid the turtledoves' endless
echo of mourning
now and then a songless angel

in a wake of ailing vultures
who remember herds
of gazelle.

EQUATION REVEALED, FIRST RELEASE, REPORTED N.Y. TIMES, NOV. 22, 2023

Today's equation is revealed:
    3 Palestinians for 1 Israeli;
    beyond the 150 for 50 exchange, 10 more

    hostages for each additional day of cease-
fire. And then there's this equation:
    1,200 Israelis killed in the first attack,

    12,000 Palestinians.
                    Is this algebra?
(And the numbers will grow

    even as) we know all men
    are created
equal.

Even with equal numbers
there is no equality of loss.
Every loss,   infinite.

Thus we're taught:
        he who saves a single life
        is regarded as creating the world.

News from the Streets

Actress Susan Sarandon says,
"Jews are getting a taste of what
it feels like to be Muslim in this country."

Muslim journalist Asra Nomai answers,
"It's an honor to live in a country
where my rights are protected."

Sarandon has cancelled filmings
for the rallies, chanting in high falsetto,
"From the river to the sea, from the river . . ."

The Gaza war continues, home and abroad.
On New York's Upper West Side by day,
posters replaced. By night, stealth-men ripping.

Over the face of one young hostage,
"Fuck you, Israel. All you
                JEWS!" scrawled
on the face of Khomkrit Chombua, 29, Thai.

Meanwhile in the U.K. . . . the O.E.D. Committee

on Redefinition meets to discuss many words
that have lost their meaning.

Crowds chanting on the streets:
                            "Genocide!"

On Redeeming Captives and a Little Known Islamic Midrash

On Oct. 18, 2011, Gilad Shalit, captive of Hamas for 5 years, was exchanged for 1,027 Palestinians, including Yahya Sinwar who underwent life-saving surgery for a brain tumor while in captivity.

The sages hold the greatest *mitzvah*—
redeeming a captive relieves hunger,
thirst, nakedness. Captives prodded
by sword point, their wounds fester

in the dark and dank, almost hidden from
G-d's all-seeing eye. Redeem them
from every prison and jail. From exile.
From all manner of torture.
                              However

captives are not to be redeemed for more
than their value. This, so it is said, will not fix
the world or lead to its betterment. Consider
Levi bar Darga, Babylonian merchant prince,

once paid 13,000 gold dinars for his daughter.
What of his cobbler, his tailor, manservant?
Could they be redeemed and not impoverish
the community?　　What of Yahya Sinwar?

During 22 years in Israeli prison he learned
perfect Hebrew, studied his enemy, prayed
five times daily for his day of revenge. There,
he prayed even more. And even more,

his forefathers were advised to pray
50 times a day, but their prophet Moses,
from a different sort of midrash,
advised reducing it to 5. Allah agreed.

What was Moshe Rabbeynu, our teacher,
and theirs, thinking? Better these cousins
remained a nation of clerics in constant prayer.
What good comes of imprisonment?

GENERATION TO GENERATION
L'dor vador

More Noas on the wall of glass,
almost all
        two hundred-forty hostages,
their faces survived the night.
The thickest tape affixes them
to the glass.
        Just one rock, one hammer,
one car in a fury
        will crash it to splinters
and the universe of faces will shatter;

the vessels of the generations in shards;

glass explodes into knives
piercing
        cheeks and brow; and there—
another Noa among them,
        they're all Noa:
Noa-Shani and Noa-
        Sahar, Noa-
            Gali
Noa-
    Eden, Noa-Hannah;
        (my Noa would make six.)

    How will we put these faces together again,

        these ripped paper faces on the sidewalk?

A Saturday Morning, Tel Aviv

My Noa's just up from a nap, calls me,
from the terrace, a WhatsApp call
so I'm right there. She carefully licks
her strawberry ice-pop, an *artic-toot*.
This one has the flavor of white inside.
"Is that vanilla or lemon?" I ask.
"White," she repeats, "it's creamy,"
and reminds me that she knows how
to make an *artic* last. "Just lick it. No
biting. Like no biting if you're mad."
She has been to the playground
with Yaav, big Adam, Tallie, and
her brother Kobi. The air was clear,
meaning sun, yes, but also no sirens.
Last week, a piece of missile fell
right onto their neighbor's terrace.
Two army men took it away.
Tomorrow, Noa's father flies to N.Y.
trusting the system to keep the air
clear for the jets' coming and going.
The children on the see-saws don't
yet know there's a system to trust
or not trust. They know the infinite
balance of up and down, pushed
and pushing. One of her friends
jumped off and Noa came thudding
down. She tells me, "I cried a little."
"That happens sometimes," I reassure
(and don't tell her that I cry a little, too.)
A few tears. But the air is clear today.

WAITING FOR THE NEXT RELEASE, REPORTED N.Y. TIMES, NOV. 23, 2023

Maybe tomorrow, if distrust
doesn't flare like a missile,
some families will be reunited.

How awful this lottery of choice;
Solomon would not deliberate.
Poster faces always before my eyes,

among them, Emma & Yuli Cunio,
twins age 3, Raz Katz-Asher, age 4,
Ariel Bibas,   another 4 year old.

What do their 4 year old minds make
            of captivity? What will they say?
      What would my Noa say?

      What will the other Noas say?
Remembering Noa Argamani, age 26,
thrown across the motorcycle

to laughter and Hamas joy.

I have almost forgotten this American day,
Thanks-
giving,

with its cornucopian harvests.
I am thinking of the cornucopian
jails of human bounty.

            (What matter now who is to blame?)

From a Graveyard for Children, a Midrash on How G-d Stopped Crying

His arms couldn't possibly hold all the dead children, and worse, His ears couldn't hold all the humming of the orphan-souls. Their melodies were mixed up and they couldn't remember their lullabies. One by one G-d whispered a musical phrase into their minds in a way they couldn't forget so they could then hear it when they breathed quietly at bedtime.

In Israel at the children's monument at Yad v'Shem, G-d gazed upon the million points of light. He could've made new light, of course, but these star-like lights were made by Man trying to live and remember after tears. He hoped Man could help with this. The more recently a child had died, the closer He drew them in, and the closer He drew them in, the more He cried.

The closest to G-d today were the children from Gaza City, but for a moment it seemed G-d couldn't tell who was from there or elsewhere, like the southern kibbutzim near Gaza. From G-d's eyes, so many tears. He wasn't seeing clearly. There were lots of child body parts and He wanted to put them back together again. The children knew who was who and didn't care. Now they had each other and hugged. It wasn't just Israeli and Palestinian children around G-d, but Ukrainians, Syrians, Hutus and Tutsi, Biafrans, and new stragglers from Darfur. In the outer rings were the children of the Shoah, as thick as the Milky Way. All the children loved the way "Milky Way" sounded, in any language.

The parents of the Shoah children were long gone and at peace, but the new Palestinian and Israeli children who stood closest to G-d would have to find their parents to console them. G-d Himself needed help for all the grieving parents. The Shoah children really understood. Sometimes there is no end to crying, but if G-d didn't stop crying, there might be another flood.

Negev heaven was very hard for children. It wasn't at all like an English meadow. It was as sharp and dry and stony as the land below, almost inhospitable. The Shoah children were especially worried about this. They knew what it was like to go barefoot on long forced marches. They drew together, discussed and argued a plan. The angels who look after children in heaven overheard and offered help.

All the shoes in the Madjanek State Museum, and all the other Holocaust Museums could help these children. The angels knew every child's shoe size, knew which to select from the many shoes in many sizes, colors, styles. Jewish shoes from across the entire Nazi Empire, long lost shoes, were brought back and given to the Shoah children who in turn found their matched Palestinian soul-mates. They passed on to them these shoes, one pair for each unsettled child-soul.

The Shoah children shuddered to remember those forced marches, but no child's bare foot could survive the Negev terrain. The newcomers, now with transported shoes on their feet, set out unhampered to find their parent or a living brother or sister or aunt. Above all, they had to help family members remember their lullabies, just as G-d had helped them.

The Shoah children knew the plan would work. G-d their Father was crying because they were crying, and they were crying because He was crying. They were all crying together. Who would stop first?

G-d felt relieved because all the comforting was now not on Him alone. Mourners could find a little more solace, especially at night remembering their family lullaby, and they woke up refreshed.

It was hard work for the children who had just died to find their families, to fill their earth-relatives with kind memories that were alive and real, and the lullabies carried a breath from heaven. The children wanted themselves to be remembered without thoughts of revenge. Their new shoes, which were old shoes, which had been on other feet, made all the difference.

(FROM CAPTIVITY) WHEN LIVING CHILDREN

return they
don't speak   they

whis-
     per   their words don't

have sound or barely enough   breath
   their words are hardly

words don't want
               to tell
what
eyes cannot unsee cannot tell in whisper-

words   their mouths move to make
whisper-sounds

                in the dark space
                of an open mouth
        where words
                    once were
            there
                is no telling a word to speak

they are ashamed
  have fled the telling
    have torn off their telling sounds
like clothes torn off
  like pieces of syllables
    cannot make words tell

                      what men
                      have done

                                    have done
                                    this

if this is man

                                              have done

A Psalm of Celebration

Thus let the redeemed of the Lord say . . .
  What can they say? They've been drugged.

Some lost their way into the wilderness.
  Some were taken into the wilderness.

In the wasteland they found no settled place
  and were settled into caves of captivity.

Some lived in deepest darkness bound in cruel irons
  that cut their wrists, their ankles.

From east and west, from north and the sea.
  From the south's inhospitable land.

He humbled their hearts.
                    Even as they resist
  humbling. How might they

Praise the Lord for his steadfast love, his wondrous deeds?
  They wait without word. Their bread is stale,

  their bruises bruised again. With broken ribs—
Praise the shatterer of bronze gates, the breaker of iron bars?

A Nightmare of Friday Evening Services
(Three Israeli hostages waving a white
flag shot dead by the IDF, Reported
N.Y. Times, Dec. 15, 2023)

The news comes at us like the bullets of a firing-squad. We shot our own? The shooter could be family. Where should we be?

> *Leave from the midst of turmoil.*

Friday late afternoon in the synagogue and we're all wandering Jews, wondering—what else should we do?

> *Long enough you sat in tears.*

Where should we sit? How should we be?

> *Lekha dodi, let us go, my beloved,*

we sing to welcome the Sabbath bride, love beyond our beloveds.

> *Shake yourself free, arise from dust.*

It is the moment when we rise to face the open door, expecting

> *Light to appear in garments of splendor,*

awaken into a different world. Singing in notes without melody. The Sabbath bride enters in tatters.   We gasp into silence.

Her organza gossamer gown ripped and bloodied. She walks past the ark, transfigures through the opposite window, staining the glass.

Far away shall be any who would devour you.

The Cantor restarts the verse which, by tradition, signals us to rise. We look again to the door. A do-over? Here-comes-the-bride again?

Another Sabbath Queen enters, then another. An entire bridal party of Sabbath Queens, all starved hostages. Their many wounds tied with strips of their gowns.

The Cantor tries to restart the verse. Louder and louder, her soprano shrills. The Rabbi holds up his hands, can't stop her:

Come O Sabbath Queen. (Aren't you) amidst the faithful of the treasured nation?

"This is not the Black Sabbath. That was October 7th. You've invited the wrong bride. Today is December 15th. Let us invoke her."

Safeguard and remember in a single utterance.

The Cantor has found her voice. She is herself again.

Come O Bride! O Shabbat Queen!

We wait   and in waiting find courage to wait.

45

Sabbath in Kurjenoff, 1901

New York was a rumor, but we knew
how to dream of Jerusalem. For centuries
we sang of next year. Desert winds rolled
each time the Torah unscrolled, roiled
in the rafters of the synagogue roof.
From huddled corners on Shabbat

we walked into Zion and home again,
our baskets full—wheat and barley
our staples, and sometimes autumnal
grapes. Sometimes figs and olives and
dates, but nothing in our imaginations
sweeter than the pomegranate. O Zion!

Not even Tsar Nicholas had seen one,
or sipped its stain of young wine—
O Zion my Zion, my harvest, my herds—
a pomegranate of a thousand seeds—
my people on the wings of a thousand
songs—

Obituary, Avrum Miles (1943-2023)

About Avrum Miles, age eighty,
who once lived in Kibbutz Be'eri.
A Hamas soldier cut his fingers off

one by one. He dies exsanguinating
in ten rivulets of blood circling
the kitchen floor. The warrior spits,

"One for each tribe of Israel."
In a whispered last call to his daughter
Avrum tells her, "*Ha-kol b'seder,* it's ok,"

and she dreams of him every night.
At first, from heaven, fingerless hands
reach down and she refuses.

She isn't ready to join him there.
One afternoon in the green vineyard
she held his younger hand. She again

takes her first steps. "*Abba sheli,*
my father," she sighs. For many nights
she searches for his fingers under the bed,

in the garden, and behind the refrigerator.
"It's ok," he tells her again, but she demands,
"Why? How? Mustn't we bury all of you?"

"Think of the vineyard," he tells her,
"each day of mourning is like a first step.
And remember . . . we are *twelve* tribes."

Two Thousand Pound Bombs Drop, Reported N.Y. Times, Dec. 22, 2023

In Khan Younis, the call to prayer
is the call of a dazed Palestinian child
crying *baba*, standing at the brim
of a cavernous pit of rubble

biting his knuckles—*baba, baba* . . .
It's so close to the *abba* of the dazed
Israeli children of Be'eri, Kfar Aza.
There is no comfort. From his uncles

he's heard the calls for revenge—
for his home and school, for his bed
of nighttime stories, for his *nana's*
whisper-song of G-d's many names.

His *Allah,* his neighbor's *Adonai,*
cry the same tears for death
and shun more blood. No miracle these
waters turning red. Who called forth

the fleets of avenging angels? By viral post:
Jewish Plagues on Gaza! A first born lost,
then a second, a third. What other plagues
pass over? Hail from the tepid sky?

From on high it falls and keeps falling.
Though we've "seen terrible things,"
will You tell us, *Adonai, Allah,* tell us—
do You remember the forgotten promise?

From the pile once home of rubble-stone,
a father's hand reaching out: *baba, abba,*
crushed by the load. We know the silence
of the lost child . . . G-d "has injured us

but will bind up our wounds . . ." Mothers
look for us, called by the name *yamma,* calling
the name *imma.* Our Father of mercy, not the god
of sacrifice.   Our many crying heads explode.

SHAME

We come to hear the mother of Naama Levy speak.
Naama still among the hostages. We're mostly Jews,
slip past the heckling crowd—

Shame, shame on you—

as if we don't hear. We hear, even inside
a battering on the door, a battering ram
against the lock, the metal twisting in—

Shame, shame on you—

sheering in shame and Naama, we know
what they've done, if she lives, is beyond
shame and her mother stops speaking—

Shame—stops her because words are what
words are, or are not, and they pierce
these walls of gathering—what is—

Shame?—and we can see the cracks,
louder words entering, between the words
the whispers of Masada, the suicides

of The Tower of York—*Shame*—less
than an echo on the city train from Vilna
to the pits in the Paneriai forest, the doors

still locked—*Shame*—in the whispers
of Poland we're locked into burning barns.

We come now to hear a mother speak without—

    Shame—

the police arrive as if to herd us off but they
say they've come to protect us from—
                                Shame—

and take us out a back door to vans of safety
and I can't remember how soon I walk through
my front door, the West End Avenue doorman's

"Good evening." I'm standing at my window
watching a tanker on the Hudson hauling what,
the refuse of what—upriver, up-time, past time,
in this time I can't help Naama. I see her with—
                                          Shame

Weaponized Sexual Violence on October 7, Reported N.Y. Times, Dec. 29, 2023

I read the article (my wife
barely able to read it) to witness,
to bear witness to the unbearable.

For weeks after, we avoid sex.

A Lesson on the Jubilee Year

Not the usual shofar trumpeting,
the *yobel*, also a ram's horn,
on this sabbath of Sabbaths,
seven cycles of seven years,
when the land itself gets a rest
from feeding a nation, indulges

in random weeds, wanton vines.
Since no one knows when again
to begin the counting, debts
accumulate, interest compounds,
servitude continues. This respite
always lives in the future, an idea.

"Why not now?" a student asks.
An old teacher clears his throat,
"All twelve tribes must reside
in the land." He's content
with his Talmud. "But where
are they then?" the child persists,

"Can't we make some new tribes?"
"New tribes?" his voice alarms, "no!
Who do you imagine they'd be?"
"Everyone who is already there!"
The teacher frowns, chokes on
dusty words stuck in his throat.

"In the Gemara there's a lost story
of the ancient rams of Mt. Moriah.
They now live on Mt. Hermon.
No one speaks their dialect.
They plead in gutturals, *Take my horn
before I die, before I die, before I die.*"

INTERROGATION

Sayid Hamas, one question
Mr. Hamas:

(You're tired. You've
trekked
home   (after,

well after, the young sister you cut
between the legs

raped the wound

(hooted and waited.
in line before   (and after

what was said?   (did you
wash the blood

from your
genitals?   (after

you'd made love to
your wife? The same
or different?   (after

your wife and the young
woman

have become blood-sisters?)

Now you become silent,
Sayid Hamas, mah ismak?

We take off your mask. Now tell us

       your name.

Israeli Military Confirmed Pulling Thousands of Troops Out of the Gaza Strip, Reported N.Y. Times, Jan. 1, 2024

This is the New Year's
news. Pulling on us
like a threat unravelling.
What else is pulling, what thread unravelling?

    The prayer shawl and the rug.

The shrug of pilling news. Or is it just
P.R? Another instagram headline?
"A low intensity campaign . . ."

    "Pockets of resistance . . ."
        they "Vowed to crush . . .
    Many soldiers

  return
to families, job, studies. Many soldiers
do not

tell what they saw, they did, the dead
do not

  watch the news that pulls us
into watching the news, unravels the threads
that clothe us, barely a tattered shirt.

  Spools of the warp and spools of the weft.

When the television goes blank.
When the computer updates dim.
Will the war ever cease?

      In the silence, the dark, dank
ghosts of the news weave their heft.   How then,

and when, can we imagine

                    peace?

In a Dream

Prison doors open but the prisoners
are confused. There are no road signs.
There are no roads.
                       Before them,
iridescent portals of light. The call to prayer
hovering in each molecule of air.

They step through into rooms of living.
A refectory table with plates of *knafeh,*
its tangy goat cheese, straws of crust
laced with rose-watered honey, platters
of strudel, sweetened tart apples and raisins
in phyllo crust, jars of milk, splitting figs.

  Families have been shuffled.
      Who belongs here?
The sentences of enemies
translate in a tingling of ears, the rush
of four-winged dragonflies, a fluttering
of words. The many songs,

the many flocks nesting in a single tree.

There are no family names, only the name
Grandmother, Grandfather, Aunt, Uncle,
Mother, Father,   but the cousin-children
don't know where   to sit, whose   hand
to trust. Among the outstretched, no hand
of comfort, these—rough, calloused, cut.

The children still walk in labyrinths
and tunnels, in the caves of collapse,
the remains of safe-rooms. They see
homes blackened with memory's splatter
no light can open.   Already these children
are exhausted,   not from what they've seen

but from what they will come to see. Not yet
born, they carry the Negev winter
daffodils, these children of buried rooms,
their pale eyes
 steadfast as the ark's eternal
light. Yes,
 these.

Conversation from New York

"I'm going again next month. You're just back. How is it?"

"Family is family. Something's changed. It's different. Hard to say. The restaurants in Tel Aviv are full. But the conversations are quiet, almost empty. Going through the motions of going through the motions. I don't know when life can return . . ."

"Forty years, my friend. Our grandchildren's lifetimes. Not ours."

BIRTHDAY

After almost a year, I return for Noa's 4th birthday.
On Hahashmonaim Street, the lone, aged trumpeter
hasn't moved from his milk-crate at the crosswalk, still
blowing a schmaltzy medley of Hatikvah and Jerusalem of
Gold, hard to decipher in his out-of-tune playing. Today
he adds a "Hello Dolly" that even Satchmo wouldn't revive.
He trumpet-nods any passer-by who notices.

In the air, a scent of strawberry and citrus, the fruit-stand near.
I buy a tub of berries, a cloud of balloons, passing him again,
ask him to the party to play ten minutes of Happy Birthday?
His place, he tells me, to remain at the crosswalk.

Children fill the party room as fast as the breezes of the day
rush through the windows, touching everything. Quick
games of tag. Noa dervishes among the children announcing
the piñata, a bird with many wings. They swat at it to bring it
to earth, and from its heavenly abdomen spills a bounty,
chocolates and gummies and pops, all now believers in

                                              what falls

from the sky,
    a louder pop, a balloon?
                          another,
a sudden silence the parents scrutinize.

                    It's nothing, nothing.

From a knot of children Noa calls out, lost in the returning
volley of voices.   A siren that can only be a siren
pierces
the room—

and a single-bodied group flows into and up the protected
stairwell, in dimmed light the siren repeats its electrical
charge that races in my spine, the realization that even as
this party began missiles were being prepared.

                    Twenty children climb the
stair-rungs like the angels in Jacob's dream who first ascend
before returning, their parents soothing them
                          only five minutes,
but this five minutes drills my mind.

                        When the all-clear
siren says to come out,
          come out of hiding, it does not

light a way
out of this war

as if we'll be hiding
in the stairwell forever

as if in that five minutes
we might hear a prophecy
that will take time out of earthly clocks.

                    How long can it take
to return from heaven?   The parents call:

    Children come back it's time, time,

and just as fast we're now singing to the sparklers
tinselling pink-frosted, sprinkle-coated cupcakes:

 Happy Birthday to you! Happy Birthday dear . . .

My daughter finds me, doesn't ask how I am or how
anyone is, holding my arm tells me this is how we go on—

 We go on.

And when the children have left and we're sweeping up
wrappers and streamers and ribbons,
         Noa, staring through
the empty room, drops to her knees then the floor. She is
filled with an immense idea.

Not a child crying, she is weeping—

Where is my birthday? Where did it go?
         Please Abba!
Please Imma! Sabba!—
     I want another birthday.

Communal Garden, Riverside Park, Free Gaza, Chalked on the Sidewalk

I should be in the mind of the park's winter
garden—a cousin dying, two friends in hospital,
the Gaza war continues. At the gate, the last
of winter waves in tattered banners of brown

hydrangea. The clematis vine plies the iron
rail, dry seedless nubs of cornflower stare,
stunned colorless. On my knees in doubt,
or prayer, I, a lone gardener, dig,

trowel-prod the packed-down patches.
Not yet planting, I prepare the soil trying
to revive its presence. Here, there, tips of
tulips pry their way out. I'll miss my friends,

our conversations. Nearby, the spent head
of a sunflower droops. Mine, too. Funerals
come and funerals pass: burials
proceed. Interruptions   of memory.

The sting recedes. Even now I   listen
for the roots, the stems, the stalks,
the worms moving within the ice-streaked
earth. In the narcissus cup, a glimpse

of a brotherly face. And in the beards
of the iris how many grandfathers will clamor
for just another hour of spring?

The Morning Call

I'm up early and call
at five-thirty or six hoping
to reach my daughter
during her lunch break.

Often we speak. If not,
the moment's mooring
moves out with the tide,
a dinghy's distant dot

in the Mediterranean
drifting to a timeless Atlantic
expanse. The phone's
ringing calls out, sounds

a Morse Code of distress.
Between rings, the silent
what-if's unformed and void
across the waters.

Prospect Park Boat House, Brooklyn

We gather on the terrace beside a park pond,
early spring, too chilly for an outdoor wedding.
The bride and groom stand beyond the weather.
He's tall and angular, like a French partisan fighter
or a Palmach soldier, today cast as a pacifist
beside his Botticelli bride, her golden brown hair
luxurious. She might have arrived in her half-shell
to this Jewish wedding. The Rabbi lifts his hands
skyward—"There, the clouds and overhanging trees,
our chuppah"—amid familiar prayers, ancient vows—
"we make our home in the world, not in our rooms."

On the arching bridge over-hung with willows,
placed on the left's perimeter, a painterly perspective,
a pack of protesters. They all shout the same words.
muffled in the distance but the rhythms of chanting
and clapping punctuate. They unfurl a banner,
hang it from the bridge: "ZionistNaziGenocide."
Clap-clap, clap-clap-clap. Stomp-stomp. Clap!

We make our home in the world, not just in our rooms.

116TH & BROADWAY

Just uptown from home, a campus
protest, a jeering crowd encamped
around *Alma Mater,* the presiding angel
of learning. I'm a by-stander, listening.
I've taught: Poetry is everywhere. Today
professors are barred from campus.

   "Jews Go Back to Poland!"

As if they want us back. The jeering crowd
pushes, enters me, joins other jeering
crowds that have slept
in the folded lobes of brain cortex
as if banished in this country's
context of freedom. *Hell no, we won't go . . .*

   "Stop Genocide Now!"

What do all the protests do? Last year
in Tel Aviv, a hundred thousand angers
and a hundred thousand prayers
every Saturday night over-filled the highway
from Kaplan Street, stopping traffic, didn't

   Stop the Crime Minister!

Here,   I'm jostled, jumped, a placard's
proclamation hits my head side-ways—
   Stay on your feet, I tell myself.

                                        Stay!
And the crowd now parts like the walls
of a once teeming Red Sea. The police
chariot through and
                                I'm swept
across the street by a sudden cross current,
by a sudden strong hand delivered
to Broadway's garden median.

        Hell no, we won't go! . . . 1968,
        Vietnam . . . *Ho-Ho- Ho Chi Minh!*
            Same rhythm, same beat . . .

            I don't ask, or can't, like Passover's
            simple son dazed by all the voices at
the table,
            drawn under the undertows of what
time
            does the tide shift, what season
passing over,

from the far side of Broadway, the ricochet
response, a counter-protest,

    "Am Yisrael Chai!"

May the people of Israel live—When the sirens
pause—May the people of Gaza live!
Here, just one broad avenue apart. Simple
rights and wrongs in bullhorns of anger
echo off these same building
                                    1969,
        napalmed children burning a poetry

of protest, the songs of Woodstock:
Richie Haven's *Freedom!*
                    FREEDOM!
Hendrix's *Star Spangled Banner. Everyday
People.* Yes, in mud and sun, wanting
change and healing and the song *Soul
Sacrifice* echoes. Who will sacrifice today?
Only demands for the sacrifice of others.

I don't know how to ask what today means.

Standing on Broadway's median in the middle
in the midst in this muddled chaos left and
right I fear I must gather my family back
to flee.   We left Egypt one people,
scattering to, and from, Iran, Iraq, from Syria,
to, and from, Europe, Russia, to and from . . .

On the median, on a bench, a hunched man
or woman, aged beyond gender, reaches
into their satchel, places a scoop of crumbs
into my hand motioning once, twice, and
together we send clouds of the bits skyward—

    whirls of white pigeons alight.

My Namesake: An Understanding
(for my grandfather)

He climbs the four story walk-up on Avenue J
his jacket held by a finger over his shoulder.
Another long day at his 5-and-10 in Brownsville.
At last he reaches Vera waiting in the doorway
too breathless to greet her. His heart seizes.   He
grips his chest. 1949, two years before I'm to be
born, I'll inherit his Hebrew name, *Asher*, happiness.
His life-line will have already threaded my veins.

I've wondered how G-d reasons: Asher/Oscar
and my Dad,   Sy,   both smokers. When armed
with school lessons, I lecture them, a ten-year-old's
new-found professorial authority: *Science has proved
smoking's bad for your health!* (Oscar's beyond listening
and Sy doesn't listen at all.) I sigh as he answers,
blowing smoke rings into the air, reducing my certainty
to doubt.
            Zeroes floating overhead,

I see my namesake peer down through the rising
clouds, whisps of his beard dangling. (Last photo,
he's clean-shaven.)
                Once G-d appeared to Moses
in a column of smoke; "spoke to Him face to face."
Moses, too, wondered about reasons, the *mishkon*
they'd build to carry forty years through the desert.
Sacrificial smoke filling space, but how can almighty
G-d of the universe, of space's far firmament, fit

inside? Many Rabbis considered the problem.
One wrote, "G-d told Moses, it's not as you think.
Build the *miskon*, as prescribed, twenty boards
on the north and south, ten on the east and west.
I will compress My *Shekhinah,* trust Me, to dwell
within it.   As it is written: *And there we'll meet
and there we'll speak."*
                         I'm gazing up through circles,
the past in circles of the future. If he hadn't smoked,

he'd have been climbing those stairs for many years,
I'd have had a different name, a different heavenly
guide mounting other stairs, ladders, bringing updrafts
of wind to his *mishkon's* inner sanctum. What's seen
in smoke—
            bless the smoke, its trailing clouds, moments
of disappearance,
                Oscar's "O", the "O" of Owen

the zeroes happily drifting into immensities.

IF THE HOLY LAND

were itself a vessel among the first
that held the world holding itself
before creation, in which was it found?

Sages conferred: Harmony, the largest, held
contraries. But Wisdom? But Knowledge?
Younger sages argued for Kindness
while those with tenure insisted, Kingship,
Majesty, or hallelujah's Crown—the *Keter*.

A peddler picking through the papers
of the proceedings came upon Endurance,
stepchild vessel, overlooked but brimming,
overflowing: Passover's phrase "next year in,"
prophetic visions, scrapped texts of Sephirot,
parchment, paper, papyrus, scrolls, pens, quills,
a surveyor's chain, zenith telescopes, map-

pieces like jig-saw puzzles, shards of the first
Endurance. Among the repaired fragments,
the duntings and crazing of many dominions
and years: here Judea and Israel, there
the walls of Rome, the floors of Istanbul,
the towers of the Crusades, the Mandate's
borders changed with wars, truces, pieces
patched, hacked, held, beheld, more lines
of repair than pieces of clay, of earth, groves,
vineyards, farms—aeons ago the sands swept
like washing waves, melding parts whole;

and so the peddler of pieces prayed: Endurance.

Rosh Hashanah Seder, 2024

I've never heard of this *Mizrahi* custom.
Celebrating with my son-in-law's family,
we're praying for something new,
almost a full year since October 7.

In this tradition, blessings are recited over:
dates, leeks, gourds, beets, apples and honey,
white beans: seven fruits and vegetables
from the market stalls. And a ram's head.

    A ram's head?

There were many heads, I was told, to choose.
Sheep or ram, horned or hornless, eyes staring up
from their moment of execution. Instead, a ram's
photo propped between the leeks and gourds.

Hezi leads the seder prayers, step by step.
Each item becomes a symbol in a linguistic twist.
Holding a date, fruit of the oasis, the word *tamar*
relates to *tam*—to "end", and we pray,

"May it be G-d's will to make an end of enemies,
of hating, of our own evil and the evil of the day."
                  Amen.

    The children declare dates too sticky.
    They're given a few gummy fish.
    A fish's head could also serve the ceremony.

Now, small white beans, fruit of the earth,
the syllables recall "many" and "heart".
The blessing, "May our merit increase,
May G-d hearten our disheartened selves."
> *Amen*

Leeks: a word related to "cut". We pray,
"May the haters and those wishing evil
be cut down in their tracks.
> *Amen, Amen,*

> The children poke at each other
> with vegetable swords.

Now we each take a beet in our palms
the size of a human heart.

> Hope's purple lump.

"May it be Your will, that those who hate,
who live by wrong-doing, depart from the land,"

> from our neighborhoods,
> keep their trucks on the road
> away from the bus-stop crowds,
> keep their knives in kitchen drawers.

"May it be Your will,"

> even if the children won't eat beets!
> They play with the gourds, odd bulbous
> twists of orange and yellow, hang them
> from shirt and shoulders, from their heads.

In the word gourd, "to rip", and "to announce."
So we pray, "Let our sins be ripped away,
our good announced."

    To the angels, if they'll listen!

And the pomegranate, fruit of fertility, its belly
filled with plush sacs of juice and seed,
"May our days be filled with many good deeds.
May our children flourish."

    And our grandchildren's children,
    let them sit between us, among us,
    taste our apples and honey. Here
    our traditions entwine across continents,

we bless and dip and pray for a sweet new year.

    But in our hearts, the beans are just
    beans, the beets, dark roots of remembrance.

And the ram? The ram! My son-in-law holds up the picture.

    The ram's pleading eyes stare, look out at us,
    one to another, searching out our guilt. Have we
    brought Yom Kippur's scape-goat to the table?

We pray, "Make us the head, not the tail, that we may lead
with righteous thought."

    Oh G-d of righteous thought, what should we
    think? When You stayed Abraham's slaying hand,

did you pity the father gripping the knife? The boy,
bound and waiting? The ram caught in the thicket
of the altar of mountain brambles?

Father of that mountain, do you pity us now?

I turn to Hezi, short for Yeheskel, grateful
he carries the traditions of his grandfather,
his namesake, Sabah Yeheskel, who had fled
Baghdad. A quiet employee in his own market
attacked him, thrust a fruit knife into his back.
Yeheskel survived. So began their exodus.
Theirs, with a million souls that year from
across North African, as far east as Afghanistan,
routed from century-old homes, beaten out,
a fraught decade after the years of human
smoke, the body exodus from Europe—

   and here we meet, ourselves

from the East and from the West,
at this family table in Ramat Gan,
near Tel Aviv, our children the link.

He turns to the children, his own,
his nieces and nephews, gathers them
near, spreads his hands over their heads
to bless them for the coming year.

  And he, how long he's been without
  his own father's blessing. And others,
  the many others left without fathers.
  I whisper the same to him as he says

"May you be like Ephraim and Manasseh . . ."

Surely like Ephraim and Manasseh . . .
May G-d preserve the strength of this
young father, holding his family dear.

Amen, Amen

"WHO WILL LAST,

what will last?" Sutzkever asks
and answers "A wind will last."
   Which wind
will last? If among the very last—

a desert wind from Sahara's mouth?
Covering houses with sand, dunes
to the doors and untended gardens,
the laundry in shreds on the line. Or,

from the lungs of the north, a scent
of gunpowder in the rain, on tomatoes
and peppers a taste of saltpeter
and charcoal, the roses sulfurous. Or,

a luminous fusion-cyclone rising
in spines, lifting earthly dwellings
into the sky.   Heaven gets further
and farther away.   Is there wind

in heaven? Beyond the clouds   wind?

A Beach in Tel Aviv

On a beach in Tel Aviv, my grandchildren chase each other into the surf's
laughter and its game of catch-me.

Ocean breezes play with the afternoon.

The clouds hover without siren break
and we don't alarm to the wings of wave-
skirting plovers, the cormorant's shadow
across the sand
              not a drone of countless
wings, not a twist of shrapnel
    falling from the iron dome.

The air stills, as if by in-held breath,

a stranger approaching. Is he lost,
come to request directions?

    "*Sabah*, Grandfather, Who is it?

Without words, he asks where and
when. If and
    when   the wind will go,

it goes,   and it goes,
    to itself, it says   go forward,
                go to yourselves.

OF SIX WINGS

Without reason, hope, we stand
on our toes three times saying
kadosh, kadosh, kadosh,
holy, holy, holy,
and stretch a few inches
up toward heaven.

Two seraphim above the arc
in unison repeat
the kadosh, singing one
to the other, *zeh l'zeh,*
from generation to generation
in pitches beyond our minds.

They each have six wings:
one pair to fly with, one pair
to cover their faces, to not look
upon the Holy of Holies.
And the third? To cover their feet?
Such a small height of our toe-rise.

It's about wings—
the stretch of fingered feathers—
the lift-off toward the cirrus clouds
beyond all conceivable expanse.
Six wings to stir the heavenly sky
and let our prayer on six wings fly!

Sutzkever's Last Words

. . . G-d will last.

Isn't that enough for you?

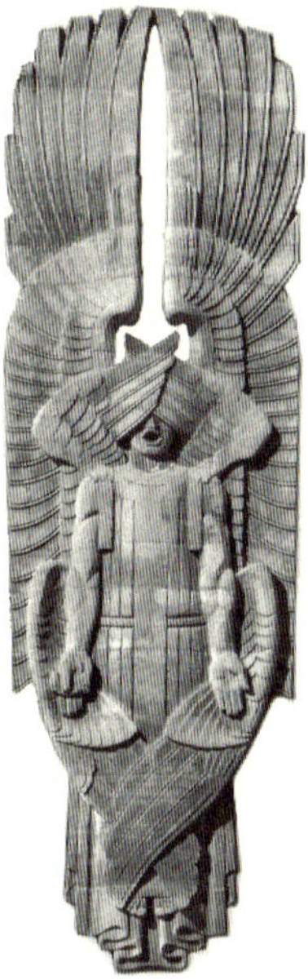

NOTES:

p.6. Kurjenoff, a village outside of Minsk (see note p. 39)

Yochevet, the mother of Moses and later Aaron and Miriam, mentioned by name in Exodus 6:20 and Num 26:59. In safety across the Red Sea, freed from Egyptian enslavement, Miriam leads the women in song and dance. (Exodus 15:20-27).

p.8. "There are not pebbles enough" references the Jewish custom of leaving a stone on a grave after visiting.

p.9. Iron Dome, the name of the early warning defense system that protects Israel from enemy missiles.

p.11. Chuppah: the wedding canopy. "Under the laws of Moses and Israel," a phrase from the traditional wedding vows. "*Hatani,*" as explained, my groom, reflecting that beyond the couple, families "marry."

The "Law of Return" guarantees citizenship in Israel for all Jews.

The image of plums "without the print of fingers" is taken from Avrom Sutskever's poem "Poetry" (1954, translated Ruth Whitman).

"I am my beloved's, my beloved, mine" is often used as a marriage vow, Song of Solomon, 6:3.

p.12. Hoopoes, the national bird. The hoopoe is the only extant members of a unique family of birds: Upupidae. It is jay-sized, with a long bill like a sandpiper's. The hoopoe's head and

85

breast are a buff pink, with a crest it can raise like a feathered headdress. Blue and white are the national colors of Israel.

p.20. *Bris,* the ritual of circumcision. A "brit" is also a promise, one of a number of promises between G-d and the Jews.

p.23. Gideon Kramer was deported to Auschwitz on Oct.1, 1944, nine days after completing his String Trio in Terezìn where he had been interred since 1941. The manuscript was entrusted to his girlfriend, Semtzka, who conveyed it to Klein's sister Eliska after the war. His sister organized the first performance of the work (outside of performances in Terezìn) in June, 1946, in Suk Hall in Prague.

Victoria Lewis, author's daughter, Assistant Concertmaster of the Israeli Opera Orchestra, has performed the Klein Trio in the Berkshires, August, 2022, New York in October, 2022, in Tel Aviv in April and June, 2023, and January, 2024. The information above derives from her introductions to each performance.

p.26. The Yom Kippur War, October 6-25, 1973.

p.29. On October 7, 2024, there were approximately 30,00 Thai nationals working in Israel, primarily in agriculture. Among the hostage were 54 Thai nationals and other individuals holding passports from 24 other countries. 31 Americans were killed in the Oct. 7 attack, and 13 presumably among the hostages.

Hagar and Ishmael: Hagar was Abraham's concubine and Ishmael his son. When Sarah conceives, she banishes them. Without water in the desert, G-d comes to their aid and provides "a skin of water. (Gen. 16:1–16; 21:8–21) Jews and Moslems share a common ancestor in Abraham and should be considered cousins.

p.32. O.E.D., Oxford English Dictionary.

p.33. From the Talmud, Gittin 45 a: 13-16; Mishnah Gittin 4:6., sources compiled by Rabbi Jeremy Kalmanofsky, Nov 25, 2023 for a weekly class at his congregation. *Mitzvah* may indicate either a good deed or the fulfillment of a commandment.

Both Jews and Moslems share Moses as a prophet. *Moshe Rabenu*, Moses our teacher (Hebrew).

p.35. *L'dor vador*, Hebrew, "in every generation," literally to generation and generation, a resonant phrase that occurs throughout the Jewish liturgy. It occurs in the Kadosh (see note p. 64) and in Passover Haggadah, "In every generation each person must see himself as having left Egypt."

p.36. *Artic* is Hebrew for icepop; *toot,* for strawberry.

p.38. A midrash is an explanation, sometimes in parable, of scripture. This poem does not expound on any specific passage, but more generally on G-d's empathy. Several citations: "I know their suffering." (Exodus 3:7) "Let my eyes run down with tears." (Jeremiah 14:17) Or, "The Lord is close to the broken-hearted." (Psalm 34:18)

Yad v'Shem is the Holocaust Museum in Jerusalem. The children's memorial is separate, commemorating the 1,000,000 children murdered in the Shoah. The memorial consists of room with a dark dome ceiling. Gradually pinpoint lights like stars come on, one million of them, a million points of light. And once they all come on, a blaze of flickering, suddenly the dome, like the heavenly sky, goes dark.

Majdanek, a Nazi concentration and extermination camp on the outskirts of Lublin, Poland, its various bunkers now museum space. Just beyond the barbed wire fencing newer apartments have been built, some with balconies facing the crematoria.

p.42. References Primo Levi's "Survival in Auschwitz" which first appeared in Italian as *"Se quest'è un uomo,"* (1947), "If This Is Man".

p.43. Psalm 107, 1-16. This psalm references the redeeming of captives.

p.44. I.D.F., Israeli Defense Force.

Italicized lines are from *Lechah Dodi,* traditionally sung at sundown to welcome the Sabbath. "Let us go, my beloved," from the Song of Songs (7:12). The text was composed in the 16th century by Shlomo Halevi Alkabetz, first of Thessalonica, then Sfat. Various communities use different melodies but the text is standard.

p.46. Kurjenoff, a village in the Minsk Gubernia (administration) currently known as Kojdanov or Koydanov. Originally settled in the 12th century, since 1801 it had been a shtetl with a significant Jewish population. Between 1897 and 1917, the Jewish population was approximately 3000, about twice its non-Jewish population. The Jewish population was allowed to trade in grain (the business of the author's great-grandmother), horses, cattle, and vodka. (https://www.jewishgen.org/belarus/lists/Economic/KOYDSUM.html)

This poem references the "seven species of the land," all native to Israel except for pomegranate.

p.48. Quotes are from Hosea: 6.

p.50. Masada: a Roman palace and fortification in the Judean desert. The Romans had expelled Jews from Jerusalem if 19 a.c.e. A group of Jews took refuge in Masada, held out for three years when, according to Josephus, 960 committed mass suicide rather than being taken as slaves to Rome.

The Tower of York (Clifford's Tower): in the 11th century 150 Jews were besieged by a mob, took refuge in the tower and committed mass suicide rather than being murdered by the mob.

The Paneriai Forest: within the city limits of Vilnius, the Russians had built and abandoned pits to construct storage for fuel. Starting in July, 1941, within months, 70,000 Jews were transported to, and exterminated in these. Also exterminated were 2,000 Poles and 8,000 Russians. When the pits filled with bodies, the Nazis burned the bodies, sent Jews into the pits to break the bones down, then sent in more Jews to be exterminated. It was an efficient place to murder most of the Jews of Vilnius since it was on a direct train line from the center of the city, only 10 kilometers away.

p.53. Jubilee Year: occurring after every seventh Sabbath year, thus, every 50 years is an economic, cultural, environmental and communal reset, when the land and people rest, and all those who are in slavery are set free to return to their communities.

p.55. *Sayid,* Arabic for "Mr." *Ma ismak,* Arabic for "What is your name?"

p.59. *Knafeh* a Palestinian dessert made with crispy shredded phyllo pastry and sweet cheese soaked in sugar syrup.

p.62. *Ha-hashmonaim* is a major street in Tel Aviv, named for the Hasmonean Dynasty established in 140 BCE after the Maccabee Revolt (167-141 BCE) by Simon, brother of Judah the Maccabee, ruling Judah and surrounding areas, until 37 BCE when the Romans under Herod displaced them. See note p. 33.

"Hatikvah," hope, Israel's national anthem. "Jerusalem of Gold" written by Naomi Shemer in 1967, just before the Six Days War at a time when entry to Jerusalem was restricted by Jordan, subsequently opened by that war. "Hello Dolly", from the 1964 Broadway play of that name. Recorded that year by Louis Armstrong (Satchmo) it became the number one hit.

Sabah is Hebrew for grandfather.

p.66. The last stanza references Genesis 2: "The earth being unformed and void (tohoo v'vohoo) with darkness over the surface of the deep and a wind from G-d sweeping over the water." (The Five Books of Moses, JPS, 2006)

p.67. The Palmach, the elite force of the Haganah, founded in 1920, the underground army of the Jewish community during the British Mandate for Palestine.

p.68. 116th Street and Broadway is the main entrance to Columbia University.

Alma Mater, the statue, sculpted by Daniel Chester French, sits in front of Columbia's Low Library overlooking the central lawn of the university.

In the 1880s and 1890s, after the assassination of Russian Tsar Alexander II, Russian-Polish Jews were exposed to a series of organized massacres targeting Jewish communities called pogroms. In response, some two millions Jews emigrated from the region, with the vast majority going to the United States.

The "simple" son in the Passover Haggadah asks, "What does this mean." The text instructs the answer, "G-d delivered us by a strong hand."

"Soul Sacrifice" performed by Santana, considered by some as the best song of the festival, and "Everday People" performed by Sly and the Family Stone at the Woodstock festival, 1969. Richie Haven's "Freedom" part of his performance that lasted nearly an hour, and Jimi Hendrix's "Start Spangled Banner" considered by some as the best performance at the festival, was the concluding act.

p.71. Mishkon, Hebrew word for the tabernacle which was transported through the desert. Described in Exodus 25:8.

Rabbi Isaiah HaLevi Horowitz (1555-1630) of Prague, then Sfat. Midrash Tanchumana, Ki Tisa 10:2.

Shekinah, Hebrew word for the presence of G-d in a place, or sometimes another word for G-d.

G-d "spoke to Moses face to face," Exodus 33:11.

p.73. References the writing of the Kabbalist, the 16th century Rabbi Isaac Luria and his idea of the ten sephirot, or vessels, of the Tree of Life. These vessels shattered when G-d's light entered the world at the moment of creation leaving divine sparks in the shards. Repair of the world, tikkun olam, involves repairing these vessels.

p.74. The prayer of blessing the eight food follows this formula, "May it be Your will, oh G-d of our fathers, that . . ." for instance, "evil, hatred, and enemies come to an end." The blessings of this seder, meaning order, follow a sequence established by Rabbi Yosef Haim of Bagdad.

"May you be like Ephraim and Manasseh" references the weekly blessing of a father to a son.

p.79. Avrom Sutzkever, poet originally from Vilna. His untitled poem begins with the lines of this book's epigram, "Who will last, what will last? A wind will last." It ends with, ". . . G-d will last.// Isn't that enough for you?" (from Twin Brother, 1986, translated Richard Fein.)

p.80. The final stanza echoes the opening of Genesis 12, "Lech lechah," usually translated as "Go forward," but also translates as "Go to yourself."

p.81. Isaiah 6:3 is the source for parts of the Kadosh, a central prayer of the service. The image of the six-winged seraphim come from this passage.

p.82. See note p.79. These are not actually Sutzkever's last words on earth, but the last words of the untitled poem that begins with the lines of the epigram.

ACKNOWLEDGMENTS:

With gratitude to the editors of the following journals who published poems from this collection, sometimes in different versions:

"Independence Day", *Minyan Magazine,* Nov 30, 2024

"(from captivity) When living children", winner of E. E. Cummings Prize, *New England Poetry Club Anthology 2024*

"My Partisan Grief, Supernova, October 7, 2023" and "A Belief in Order", *Witnessing Series, Jewish Book Council,* posted October 7, 2024.

"Weaponized Sexual Violence in Gaza, Reported December 29, 2023", *Lilith,* Spring 2025.

"At-Home Coliseum, New York", "Obiturary, Avram Miles (1943-2023)", "Sabbath in Kurjinoff, 1901", *arc 31,* December, 2024.

"A Lesson on the Jubilee Year", "If the Holy Land", and "Of Six Wings", *Lehrhaus,* December 23, 2024

"The Doves of Ma'agan", *Poetry News* (December, 2024) as a selection in the Poetry Society's (U.K.) winter competition.

ABOUT THE AUTHOR:

OWEN LEWIS is the author of four collections of poetry and three chapbooks. Honors include the 2024 E.E.Cummings Prize, the 2023 Guernsey International Poetry Prize, the 2023 Rumi Prize for Poetry, the International Hippocrates Prize for Poetry and Medicine, and the Jean Pedrick Chapbook Award. At Columbia University he is Professor of Psychiatry in the Department of Medical Humanities and Ethics and teaches Narrative Medicine.

Author photo by Francesco Barascuitti

Other books by Owen Lewis
published by Dos Madres Press

Sometimes Full of Daylight (2013)
best man (2015)
Marriage Map (2017)
Field Light (2020)
Knock-*Knock* (2024)

He is also included in:
Realms of the Mothers:
The First Decade of Dos Madres Press - 2016

For the full Dos Madres Press catalog:
www.dosmadres.com